Top 10 Worst ™

Wicked Rulers

you wouldn't want to know!

Gareth Stevens
Publishing

Please visit our Web site, **www.garethstevens.com**. For a free color catalog of all our high-quality books, call toll free 1-800-542-2595 or fax 1-877-542-2596.

Library of Congress Cataloging-in-Publication Data

Macdonald, Fiona, 1958-
Top 10 worst wicked rulers / Fiona Macdonald.
    p. cm. - (Top 10 worst)
Includes index.
ISBN 978-1-4339-6701-6 (pbk.)
ISBN 978-1-4339-6702-3 (6-pack)
ISBN 978-1-4339-6700-9 (library binding)
1. Kings and rulers-Biography-Juvenile literature. 2. Heads of state-Biography-Juvenile literature. I. Title. II. Title: Top ten worst wicked rulers.
D107.M295 2012
321.0092'2-dc23
                              2011022850

First Edition

Published in 2012 by
Gareth Stevens Publishing
111 East 14th Street, Suite 349
New York, NY 10003

© 2012 The Salariya Book Company Ltd

Series creator: David Salariya
Editor: Stephen Haynes
Illustrations by David Antram

Printed in Heshan, China

CPSIA compliance information: Batch #SW12GS: For further information contact Gareth Stevens, New York, New York at 1-800-542-2595.

Top 10 Worst

Wicked Rulers

you wouldn't want to know!

Illustrated by
David Antram

Written by
Fiona Macdonald

Created & designed by
David Salariya

3

Contents

Not nice to know!

Kings, queens, princes, chieftains, mighty emperors and scheming politicians—at different times and in different places, they've all been terrible rulers. In past grim and bloodstained centuries, rulers have been bad in many different ways: lazy, greedy, cruel, corrupt, bungling, bigoted, vicious or—sometimes—tragically insane…

So beware, as you travel back in time to meet them! These people were dangerously tough, determined, and ruthless—definitely not nice to know!

King Richard III (England, ruled 1483–1485) murdered his two young nephews, the "Princes in the Tower," in his bid to become king.

Emperor Yang (China, ruled AD 604–618) sent 5 million men to dig great canals; almost half died.

King Philip III (Spain, ruled 1598–1621) drove 300,000 Moriscos (Spanish Muslims) out of Spain at gunpoint.

Queen Fredegund (France, lived AD 550–597) made her husband kill his first wife, then plotted and killed to make her son king.

5

What made them wicked?

Some rulers had wild ambitions and would stop at nothing to achieve them. Some were driven to dreadful deeds by extreme religious or political beliefs. Others killed, imprisoned, or tortured to make their nations great, win worldwide fame, drive out invaders, or conquer more land. Many used terror to get—and keep—power for their own dynasties. No one dared stop them.

Some past rulers may not have committed all the terrible crimes they've been accused of. But their fame has lasted centuries, as a lesson for all of us in how *not* to behave.

So many ways to be bad...

Legends tell how noble warrior Macbeth (lived c. 1040) believed a prophecy that one day he'd rule Scotland. So he murdered Scotland's king, rival nobles, and a whole family of innocent children. But their ghosts came to haunt him.

Jezebel

In ancient Israel, around 850 BC, Queen Jezebel killed Jewish leaders and built temples to foreign gods. As punishment, she was thrown out of a window and her body was eaten by dogs.

Macbeth and the ghost of Banquo

Bad or brave?

Francisco Solano López (1826–1870) was president of Paraguay, South America. To keep hold of power, he killed hundreds of politicians and church leaders—and even his own brothers and brothers-in-law. He was a bold, fearless warrior but by the time he died, Paraguay was poor, weak, and defeated.

Francisco Solano López

Remorseful ruler

King Ashoka the Terrible of India (304–232 BC) was a fierce and famous warrior. But he became shocked and sickened by slaughter and suffering. At the end of one bloody battle, he exclaimed in horror: "What have I done? Is this really victory?"—and vowed to work for peace for the rest of his life.

Horrid Herod

Herod the Great, King of Israel (c. 73 BC–4 BC), feared that rivals would seize his throne—so he gave orders that his wife, two of his sons, and many religious leaders who criticized him should be killed. According to the Christian Bible, Herod ordered the slaughter of all the baby boys born in Bethlehem around the same time as Jesus Christ.

Herod the Great

A world of wickedness

All around the world, stories have been told about wicked rulers who lived long ago. But who decided what was good or bad about them? Dead rulers' life histories were often rewritten by their enemies, with the hope of disgracing them—forever. New rulers also spread false rumors about kings and queens they had overthrown, to explain—and excuse—their own violent actions.

Hero or villain? Or both?

A ruler's reputation might also depend on whether they were successful. Had they won battles? Conquered land? Made their country rich and powerful? If so, people living at the time, and later historians, might overlook their dreadful deeds and call them not wicked, but heroic.

8

1. Nero
2. Leopold II
3. Vlad Țepeș
4. Ivan the Terrible
5. The first Chinese emperor
6. Maximilien Robespierre
7. King John
8. Cleopatra
9. Henry VIII
10. Erik Bloodaxe

4

Remember—
history is written
by the winners!

5

N

Ruthless recent rulers?

Sadly, yes, there have been
many! Probably more
people in modern times
have suffered because of
wicked rulers than at any
time in the past. But these
modern rulers and their
crimes are too close to
us—and to their victims.
We must let future
generations judge them.

Nº 10

Erik Bloodaxe

Erik Bloodaxe! His name says it all. Even for violent Vikings, Erik was a bit too bloodthirsty. Born in Norway, he became a Viking pirate at just 12 years old. Then he killed four of his own brothers to make sure that he became king. But Erik was a cruel and unjust ruler, so the Norwegians (plus a brave surviving sixth brother) drove him out.

Vital statistics

Name: Erik Haraldsson
Nickname: Bloodaxe
Born: Norway
Ruled: Norway c. AD 931–933; Jorvik c. 947–948 and 952–954
Career: Pirate, king
Dreadful deeds: Killing and raiding
Died: Killed at Stainmore, near Durham, England

You wouldn't want to know this:

Erik's wife Gunnild was trained as a witch. People said she could fly, and she certainly could concoct some very nasty poisons. She was eventually punished by being drowned in a bog.

They don't call me "Bloodaxe" for nothing!

Be prepared!
Always expect the very worst

Treasure seeker

Erik sailed vast distances, attacking people from Russia to Scotland, and maybe as far south as Spain. He wanted gold, silver, and captives to sell as slaves.

Too rough!

For ten years Erik robbed and raided as a pirate. Then he sailed south and took control of Jorvik (York) in northern England. But his brutal rule shocked the citizens, and they plotted with rival rulers to murder him.

Nasty surprise!

Driven out of Jorvik, Erik was attacked and killed by Scottish warriors. Was it a planned ambush? Yes, probably!

Another vicious Viking

The Normans were Viking raiders who settled in France. In 1066, they invaded England, led by Duke William (later known as "the Conqueror"). When the northern English rebelled, William set fire to their houses and crops, and destroyed their goods, tools, and weapons. Countless families starved to death, and the land did not recover for 100 years.

Tremble!

No 9

Henry VIII

H andsome, athletic, and well-educated, young Henry was praised as the "ideal prince." But by the time he died—at only 55—he had become a royal monster: surly, spiteful, suspicious, stubborn, selfish, unpredictable, and hot-tempered. He was a dangerous friend, and a deadly enemy. Around 72,000 people were put to death during his reign.

Thomas More d. 1535

Thomas Cromwell d. 1540

Anne Boleyn d. 1536

Vital statistics

Name: Henry Tudor
Nickname: Great Harry
Born: England
Ruled: 1509–1547
Career: King of England; head of the new Church of England
Dreadful deeds: Had thousands of opponents and two of his six wives executed
Died: In bed, of disease

You wouldn't want to know this:

By the time Henry died, his waist measured 54 inches (137 cm).

They dare to displease me! They must die!

Be prepared!
Always expect the very worst

Katherine of Aragon

Anne Boleyn

Jane Seymour

Anne of Cleves

Katherine Howard

Katharine Parr

Divorced, beheaded, died, divorced, beheaded, survived

The search for a son

Henry needed a male heir to rule after him. So he married again and again – but only his last, childless marriage was happy.

Fallen hero

In 1536, Henry fell from his horse during a joust (mock battle). The blow on the head made him depressed and bad-tempered for the rest of his life.

Nnngh

Katherine Howard d. 1542

Edward Stafford d. 1521

Cardinal Thomas Wolsey d. 1530

Bloody Mary

Henry VIII's oldest daughter, Mary I (ruled 1553–1558), was every bit as determined as her father. But, unlike him, she did not want the Church in England to be independent from the Roman Catholic Church. She executed over 300 Protestant men and women who did not share her Catholic beliefs.

Off with their heads!

King Henry was ruthless about getting his own way. His wives and advisors stayed safe only while they pleased him. Disobedience might mean death!

No 8

Cleopatra

Beautiful but deadly—and maybe misunderstood—Cleopatra was the last queen to rule ancient Egypt. She lost a mighty kingdom, saw her people starve—and fell in love with two enemy Roman generals. Did she neglect her country to follow the men she loved? Or did she use her beauty and charm to try to stop the Romans from invading? If she did, she failed. After 3,000 glorious years, proud, rich Egypt was conquered by Rome in 30 BC.

Hidden charms

In 48 BC, Roman commander Julius Caesar arrived in Egypt. Cleopatra was afraid that her brother would kill her so that he could rule alone, so she smuggled herself into Caesar's room to ask for his protection.

Vital statistics

Name: Cleopatra VII Philopator
Nicknames: Great Lady of Perfection, Queen of Kings
Born: Egypt
Ruled: 51–30 BC
Career: Queen of Egypt
Dreadful deeds: Arranging family murders
Died: Suicide, by snakebite or poison

You wouldn't want to know this:

Cleopatra spent a fortune on clothes and feasts, while many Egyptians were poor and hungry.

Surprise!

Bewitching!

Be prepared!
Always expect the very worst

Family matters

Caesar and Cleopatra fell in love—and Cleopatra's brother was found dead. Suspicious deaths happened all too often in Cleopatra's family: both her brothers and all three of her sisters died before her, either executed or murdered.

Bearded lady

Not everyone approved of female rulers. To show that she was just as good as a man, Egyptian Queen Hatshepsut (ruled 1508–1458 BC) wore a false beard, a traditional sign of kingly power.

You look divine, dear

Caesar paid for a gold statue of Cleopatra looking like Isis, the Egyptian goddess of life and love. Roman priests and people were shocked.

Death—and dishonor

Caesar helped Cleopatra stay in power. But he was murdered in 44 BC. Now who would protect her? In 41 BC, Cleopatra fell in love with a second Roman leader, Mark Antony. Together they planned to rule Egypt and conquer a vast empire, free from Roman control. However, their army was defeated in 31 BC. In disgrace and despair, they killed themselves.

Who, me?*

15

*Some say that Cleopatra committed suicide by teasing a poisonous snake until it bit her.

No 9

King John

The only king of England to be nicknamed "bad," John was short, stout, richly dressed, and very fond of women—and luxuries. John passed harsh new laws, grabbed land and treasures, mocked the Church, and did nothing to help poor, ordinary people. Worst of all, his disastrous wars lost rich English lands in France— and he threatened the ancient legal rights of his subjects.

Vital statistics

Name: John Plantagenet
Nicknames: Lackland, Softsword
Born: England
Ruled: 1199–1216
Career: Lord of Ireland, Prince in Aquitaine (western France), King of England
Dreadful deeds: Greedy and unjust; his wars lost half a kingdom
Died: Of dysentery

You wouldn't want to know this:

When John lost his temper, he would gnaw his fingers in fury.

Lost in the Wash

In 1216, King John became ill while traveling. He went back to bed (where, in 6 days, he died). But he sent his horses, loaded with favorite royal jewels, by a shortcut over a marshy bay known as the Wash. Trapped by the tide, the horses drowned and the jewels were lost.

Be prepared!
Always expect the very worst

Magna Carta

John's harsh rule made the barons (nobles) angry. In 1215, they drew up a Great Charter—a list of their demands. The most important: no imprisonment without trial, and no new taxes unless the barons were consulted.

> I'll sign it, but I won't stick to it.

> That'll teach him!

Birth of a legend?

Stories about outlaw hero Robin Hood may have started after King John gave new powers to royal officials such as sheriffs. Poor people complained that John's officials were cruel, greedy, and unjust—and the Sheriff of Nottingham became Robin's great enemy.

Expensive tastes

King John needed cash—to pay for his wars, his castles, his jewels, his fine clothes, and his girlfriends. He also gave expensive gifts to his friends, to make sure they kept on supporting him. How did he get the money? By raising taxes, and sending fierce tax collectors all around his kingdom.

> Hand it over!

You're banned!

John wanted to name his own Church officials, but the Pope insisted this was *his* duty. To punish John, the Pope placed England under an interdict (religious ban), which meant that no one could marry or hold a funeral. Ordinary people were very upset—and furious with John.

17

No 6

Maximilien Robespierre

"The King must die!" shouted angry mobs in the streets of Paris, France. In 1789, they launched a revolution to get rid of King Louis XVI and win power for themselves. From 1793 to 1794, Robespierre was their leader. Around 40,000 "enemies of the state"—including most of the royal family—were killed during his bloody Reign of Terror.

Guillotine

Vital statistics

Name: Maximilien François Marie Isidore de Robespierre

Nickname: The Incorruptible*

Born: France

Lived: 1758–1794

Career: Lawyer, then revolutionary

Dreadful deeds: Led bloodthirsty Reign of Terror

Died: Executed by guillotine

You wouldn't want to know this:

He tried to kill himself the night before his execution. He was probably scared by stories of victims' heads that went on living and feeling pain after they had been cut off.

*Incorruptible: always honest

Be prepared!
Always expect the very worst

Word power

Robespierre won support for the French Revolution by making rousing speeches, and by his pure and honest lifestyle. But his ideas became dangerously extreme. He thought terror and bloodshed were the only way to run the new revolutionary government. After a year as leader, he was condemned to die.

What about the workers?

The revolution of 1789 began with protests by poor, starving workers. Their lives were hard and they paid heavy taxes, while French royalty—especially pretty, silly Queen Marie Antoinette—led lives of luxury. Royalty had to go!

They have no bread? Let them eat cake!

Liberty, equality, fraternity—or death!

Out of control

During Robespierre's Reign of Terror, thousands of Paris citizens were guillotined. But thousands more nobles, priests, government officials, and ordinary people were killed by angry mobs in the countryside. Robespierre could not stop the mass slaughter he had started. The revolution was out of control!

No 5

The first Chinese emperor

Qin Shi Huangdi was the first man to unite the warring states of China and create one huge Chinese empire. The Great Wall he ordered to defend his country is one of the Wonders of the World. So is his secret tomb, guarded by the famous Terracotta Army. But countless millions died working on his massive building schemes.

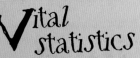

Vital statistics

Name: Prince Ying Zheng
Title: Qin Shi Huangdi*
Born: Kingdom of Qin
Ruled: Qin, 246–221 BC; all of China, 221–210 BC
Career: First ruler of all of China
Dreadful deeds: Executed many enemies; millions died working for him
Died: From taking mercury pills, which he hoped would make him live forever.

You wouldn't want to know this:

Afraid of dying, he sent explorers to search for the magic Elixir of Life. They never found it, of course, but dared not return to tell him.

First All-Powerful Chinese Emperor

They call this Wall the biggest tomb in the world— so work until you die!

20

Be prepared!
Always expect the very worst

Burning books

Qin Shi Huangdi wanted to keep firm control of his new empire. So he ordered fine new coins, weights and measures, new roads, canals, ships and wagons, and a new way of writing. He outlawed writers and thinkers, burned books he disagreed with, and buried scholars alive.

Last empress

Ambitious, determined—and beautiful—Cixi was the very last empress of China. She ruled on behalf of her young son Tongzhi (1861–1874), and then for his cousin Guangxu (1875–1908). Some call her corrupt and greedy. Others say that she did her best to protect the ancient Chinese empire during very difficult times.

I demand immortality!

Death mission

When Qin Shi Huangdi died, his courtiers were afraid to tell anyone. So they carried his decaying body for many miles to his tomb, followed by a cartload of rotting fish to disguise the smell. Once the emperor was safely buried, nearly all the tomb workers were killed, so that they would not reveal the secrets of the tomb.

Fish cart

20

No 4

Ivan the Terrible

Vital statistics

Name: Ivan IV Vasilyevich
Nickname: Grozny (Terrible or Awesome)
Born: Moscow, Russia
Ruled: 1533–1584
Career: First tsar of Russia
Dreadful deeds: Massacred his own subjects
Died: Possibly murdered

You wouldn't want to know this:

It was rumored that Ivan's secret police carried real dead dogs' heads to terrify their enemies.

At first, Ivan IV's reign was glorious. He reformed the government and the law; paid for wonderful new buildings; encouraged art, craft, and trade; and conquered Siberia. But as Ivan grew older, his behavior changed. Was he ill? Or mad? Being slowly poisoned? Or just wicked?

Ivan quarreled with the people of Novgorod. He declared that he was the punishing "Hand of God," and gave orders for them all to be killed. Around 60,000 died.

Be prepared!
Always expect the very worst

Cruel reward

Tsar Ivan paid for the best architect in Russia to design an amazing new cathedral for Moscow. According to legend, when the building work was done, Ivan had the architect blinded so that he could never build anything better.

St. Basil's Cathedral

Unfair, unfree

Ivan took away the freedom of the Russian peasants (farmworkers). They became serfs—almost slaves. Farmers actually owned them, like animals.

The Tsar's Dogs

Ivan created a new and terrible secret police force, the *Oprichniki*. Nicknamed "the Tsar's Dogs," they spied on the Russian people and were free to murder, burn, loot, and destroy.

Nobody expects the *Oprichniki*.

Death comes home

Ivan brutally beat his son's wife, because he thought her clothes were immodest. Ivan's son tried to defend her—but his father's big stick hit him on the head. Ivan's son died, and his wife lost the baby she was expecting—a double tragedy.

23

№o 3

Vlad Țepeș

IF, IF, IF all the reports about Prince Vlad are true, he must have been one of the most wicked rulers ever. But many of the worst tales were told by his enemies, who may have exaggerated them. We do know, however, that Vlad fought bravely to defend his homeland against invaders—and killed his enemies in a very cruel and revolting way.

Vital statistics

Name: Vlad III, Prince of Wallachia
Nicknames: Vlad Țepeș (Vlad the Impaler), Vlad Dracula
Born: Transylvania*
Ruled: 1448, 1456–1462, 1476
Career: Warlord and ruler
Dreadful deeds: Mass murder and torture
Died: In battle, fighting invading Ottoman Turks

You wouldn't want to know this:

It was rumored that Vlad skinned, boiled, and roasted enemy captives— then force-fed their flesh to their families.

then in Hungary, now in Romania

Hero and monster— that's me!

24

Be prepared!
Always expect the very worst

Vampire name, vampire nature?

Dracula—Dragon's Son—that's what they called Vlad. His father's nickname had been "Dragon"—and Vlad was just as dangerous! Many years later, in 1896, Irish novelist Bram Stoker used Dracula as the name for his bloodthirsty vampire villain. It became famous worldwide.

But was the real Vlad a vampire? No!

A terrible warning

Vlad's favorite way of killing people was by impaling—hammering huge wooden stakes through them. Why was he so cruel? Because he wanted to bring law and order to his homeland, and keep enemies away. He hoped that his brutal executions would terrify criminals and invaders.

Vlad also killed to end the power of ancient noble familes; he feared they might rebel against him. So he forced top noblemen to build his new castle. They had to work—naked—until they collapsed and died.

It's war!

Vlad spent years fighting Turkish invaders. He even attacked peaceful messengers sent by Turkey to his court. Grimly, he joked that they'd been slow to show him respect by removing their turbans. So he murdered them by nailing the hats to their heads.

25

No 2

Leopold II

In the 19th century, powerful European nations grew rich from trading with their overseas colonies. Belgium had no colonies, but King Leopold II wanted an empire of his own. In 1885, he paid soldiers and explorers to take control of the Congo region* in Africa. He made a fortune from trade—but treated African people with appalling cruelty.

A British cartoon of the time showed Leopold as a snake crushing an African.

Vital Statistics

Name: Léopold Louis Philippe Marie Victor; Leopold II of Belgium
Born: Belgium
Ruled: 1865–1909
Career: King of Belgium
Dreadful deeds: Killing and exploiting African people; denying their human rights
Died: Of old age, safely at home in Belgium

You wouldn't want to know this:

By the end of his life, Leopold was so unpopular that his funeral procession was booed.

26

*now the Democratic Republic of Congo

Be prepared!
Always expect the very worst

Savage slavery

The Congo Free State (as it was called) belonged to Leopold himself, not to Belgium. If Leopold's African slave workers did not supply enough ivory or rubber, he had their hands cut off. Others were beaten so badly that they died. Probably half the people in the Congo Free State were killed, or died of hunger and sickness, during Leopold's reign.

Something must be done

In 1904, missionaries set up the Congo Reform Association to tell the world about the shocking abuses there. The British government ordered a report on the subject. The news of Leopold's cruelty caused international outrage, and in 1908 the Belgian government took over control of the Congo. It became an independent country in 1960.

A delicate matter

King Leopold was a close relative of Britain's Queen Victoria. So, while she lived, the British government found it difficult to criticize his terrible crimes. But as soon as Victoria died, in 1901, British politicans felt free to speak out.

Congo Free State

Scramble for Africa

Between 1881 and 1914, rival European nations competed greedily to grab vast areas of land in Africa. They wanted Africa's rich resources: gold, diamonds, copper, rubber, and ivory.

27

Nero

Too much, too young! Nero became Roman emperor—the mightiest ruler in the western world—when he was only 17. The power quickly went to his head. Desperate to win popularity with the Roman people, he ignored wise advice, spent government money wildly, and provoked rebellion against his rule. Worst of all, he seems to have greatly enjoyed killing anyone who displeased him.

Vital statistics

Birth name: Lucius Domitius Ahenobarbus
Name as emperor: Nero Claudius Caesar Augustus Germanicus
Born: Rome, Italy
Ruled: AD 54–68
Career: Roman emperor
Dreadful deeds: Murdered his family and political rivals, persecuted Christians
Died: Killed himself to escape assassination

You wouldn't want to know this:

Nero may have started a massive fire that wrecked half of Rome, just to clear space for his new palace.

> They say I played music while Rome burned—not true!

Be prepared!
Always expect the very worst

Horrid husband

Nero divorced his first wife, exiled her from Rome, then had her executed when she returned. When Nero's second wife suddenly collapsed and died, people said that he had kicked her to death.

Bloodstained dynasty

In AD 54, Nero's mother, Agrippina, killed Nero's stepfather, Emperor Claudius, so that Nero could seize power. The next year, Nero poisoned his teenage stepbrother Britannicus, who had more of a right to rule. Then, in AD 59, Nero killed his own mother. He suspected she was plotting against him.

No contest

No one criticized Nero and survived! He killed countless people who complained about his policies. He forced everyone to applaud when he sang in public. He insisted on competing in chariot races at the Olympic Games, and made sure the judges declared him the winner.

Tra-la!

Thrown to the lions

Nero thought Christians were a threat to Roman power, so he had them killed in extremely nasty ways—by burning them alive, crucifying them, feeding them to ravenous dogs, using them as bait for wild beasts in the arena, or making them fight trained gladiators.

Glossary

Arena A large, open-air space surrounded by seats; used for sports contests, concerts, and (in Roman times) gladiator fights.

Assassination Murder by enemies, especially the murder of a political leader.

Colony A land conquered and ruled by a stronger nation.

Courtier A member of a noble family, or a government official, who works (and often lives) at a ruler's court as a companion and advisor.

Crucify To kill by nailing to a wooden cross.

Dynasty A series of rulers who all belong to the same family.

Dysentery An infectious disease that causes serious diarrhea. It can be fatal if modern medicines are not available.

Elixir A magic potion.

Exile To force a person to leave their homeland.

Exploit To make unfair use of.

Gladiator A person—often a slave, criminal, or member of a religious minority—who was forced to fight to the death to entertain crowds in ancient Rome.

Guillotine A machine designed to cut off human heads quickly and efficiently. It consisted of a sharp metal blade in a wooden frame.

Heir A person who inherits (or will inherit) a title or property from someone who has died.

Human rights Rights such as safety, justice, and freedom, belonging equally to all human beings.

Ivory A valuable, smooth, white, shiny substance taken from the tusks of elephants. It was used for jewelry and works of art. The supply is now strictly controlled.

Magna Carta (Great Charter) An important legal document: a set of rules for royal good behavior that the English barons (noblemen) forced King John to agree to in 1215.

Massacre The killing of a large number of people.

Ottoman The name of a Turkish dynasty and the empire it ruled in Europe and the Middle East from 1299 to 1922.

Persecute To seek out a particular group of people and harm or kill them.

Prophecy Words that are believed to foretell the future.

Protestant A member of the reformed branch of the Christian Church.

Revolutionary A person who plans or takes part in a plot to overthrow a ruler or a government.

Roman Catholic A member of the branch of the Christian Church led by the Pope in Rome.

Serf A poor farmworker who had no freedom and very few rights. Serfs belonged to landowners, almost like farm animals.

Tax Money which citizens have to pay to rulers or governments; it is used to defend and run their country.

Tsar The ruler of Russia and its empire. (The title is a Russian version of the Roman name "Caesar.")

Warlord A ruler who controls an area by military force alone.

Index